Hammer

Creative Education

SWIMMERS

On The Cover:
An Ancient Armored Fish.
The first vertebrates—animals with
backbones—were fish.
Cover Art by Walter Stuart.

Published by Creative Education, Inc., 123 South Broad Street, Mankato, Minnesota 56001

Printed by permission of Wildlife Education, Ltd.

ISBN 0-88682-390-0

Created and written by
John Bonnett Wexo

Chief Artist
Walter Stuart

Senior Art Consultant
Mark Hallett

Design Consultant
Eldon Paul Slick

Production Art Director
Maurene Mongan

Production Artists
Bob Meyer
Fiona King
Hildago Ruiz

Photo Staff
Renee C. Burch
Katharine Boskoff

Publisher
Kenneth Kitson

Associate Publisher
Ray W. Ehlers

SWIMMERS

This Volume is Dedicated to: Melissa, Marie and Amy Wexo, my daughters, who have given me joy in their talents and their achievements.

Art Credits

Page Eight: Upper Right and Lower Left, Colin Newman; Pages Eight and Nine: Lower Center, Walter Stuart; Page Nine: Walter Stuart; Page Ten: Far Left, Robert Bampton; Pages Ten and Eleven: Upper Center, Robert Bampton; Middle, Colin Newman; Page Eleven: Walter Stuart; Page Twelve: Upper Middle and Lower Left, Colin Newman; Middle Right, Robert Bampton; Page Thirteen: Walter Stuart; Page Fourteen: Left, Walter Stuart; Right, Colin Newman; Page Fifteen: Top, Walter Stuart; Middle Right, Colin Newman; Lower Right, Walter Stuart; Page Sixteen: Middle Left, Walter Stuart; Lower Left, Robert Bampton; Upper Right, Robert Bampton; Pages Sixteen and Seventeen: Center, Colin Newman; Page Seventeen: Top and Middle Right, Walter Stuart; Bottom, Robert Bampton; Page Eighteen: Left, Walter Stuart; Pages Eighteen and Nineteen: Center, Colin Newman; Page Nineteen: Top and Lower Left: Walter Stuart; Lower Right, Colin Newman; Page Twenty: Timothy Hayward; Page Twenty-one: Colin Newman; Lower Right, Robert Bampton; Pages Twenty-two and Twenty-three: Background, Timothy Hayward; Figures: Chuck Byron.

Photographic Credits

Pages Six and Seven: Gordon Menzie (Model by Walter Stuart); Page Eight: Garth Ware; Page Eleven: Gordon Menzie (Puzzle by Walter Stuart); Page Fourteen: Jeff Rotman (Peter Arnold, Inc.); Page Fifteen: Upper Middle, Gordon Menzie; Lower Middle, Jeff Rotman (Peter Arnold, Inc.); Lower Left, Menzie Photography (Carina Schoening); Lower Right, Menzie Photography (Carina Schoening); Page Sixteen: Gordon Menzie; Page Eighteen: Zig Leszczynski (Animals Animals).

Creative Education would like to thank Wildlife Education, Ltd., for granting them the right to print and distribute this hardbound edition.

Contents

Animals without backbones evolved into animals with backbones.

Swimmers

For 3 billion years, the only animals on the earth were **invertebrates**—animals without backbones. All of them lived in the water. Most of them lived on the bottom of the ocean. And some lived in fresh water. Then, about 500 million years ago, the first animals with backbones appeared—the **vertebrates**. The backbone was a very important "invention" of evolution. And scientists have an interesting theory about where it came from . . .

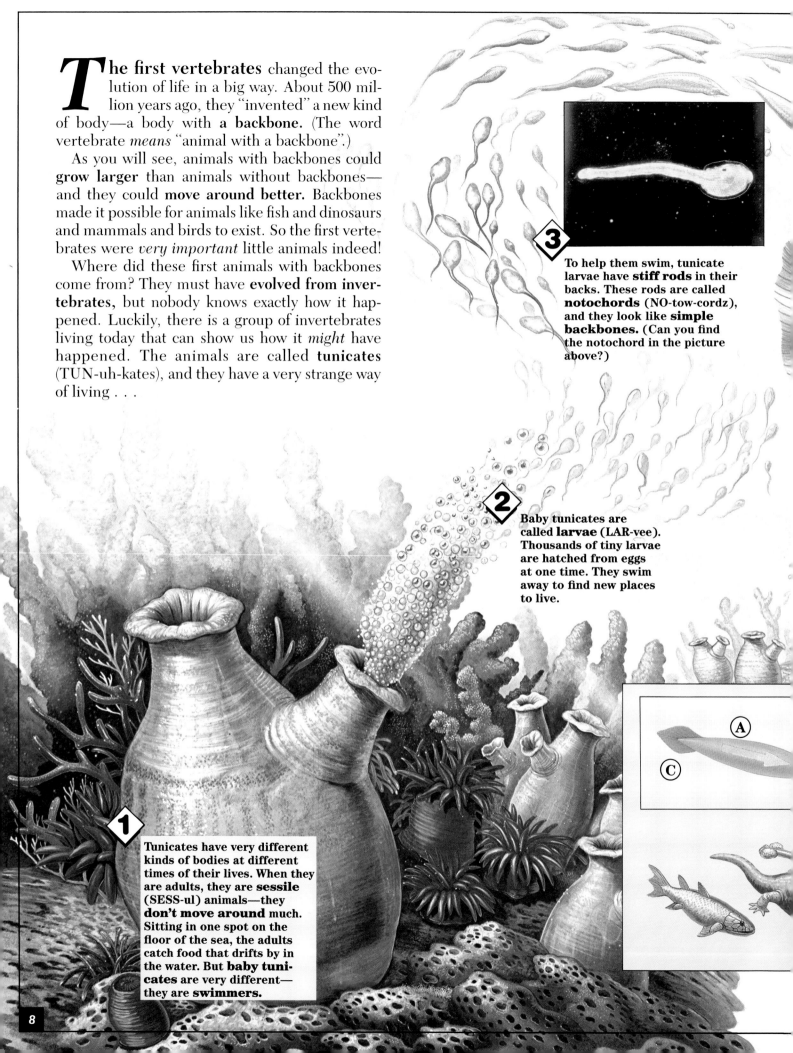

The first vertebrates changed the evolution of life in a big way. About 500 million years ago, they "invented" a new kind of body—a body with **a backbone.** (The word vertebrate *means* "animal with a backbone".)

As you will see, animals with backbones could **grow larger** than animals without backbones—and they could **move around better.** Backbones made it possible for animals like fish and dinosaurs and mammals and birds to exist. So the first vertebrates were *very important* little animals indeed!

Where did these first animals with backbones come from? They must have **evolved from invertebrates,** but nobody knows exactly how it happened. Luckily, there is a group of invertebrates living today that can show us how it *might* have happened. The animals are called **tunicates** (TUN-uh-kates), and they have a very strange way of living . . .

3 To help them swim, tunicate larvae have **stiff rods** in their backs. These rods are called **notochords** (NO-tow-cordz), and they look like **simple backbones.** (Can you find the notochord in the picture above?)

2 Baby tunicates are called **larvae** (LAR-vee). Thousands of tiny larvae are hatched from eggs at one time. They swim away to find new places to live.

1 Tunicates have very different kinds of bodies at different times of their lives. When they are adults, they are **sessile** (SESS-ul) animals—they **don't move around** much. Sitting in one spot on the floor of the sea, the adults catch food that drifts by in the water. But **baby tunicates** are very different—they are **swimmers.**

A

C

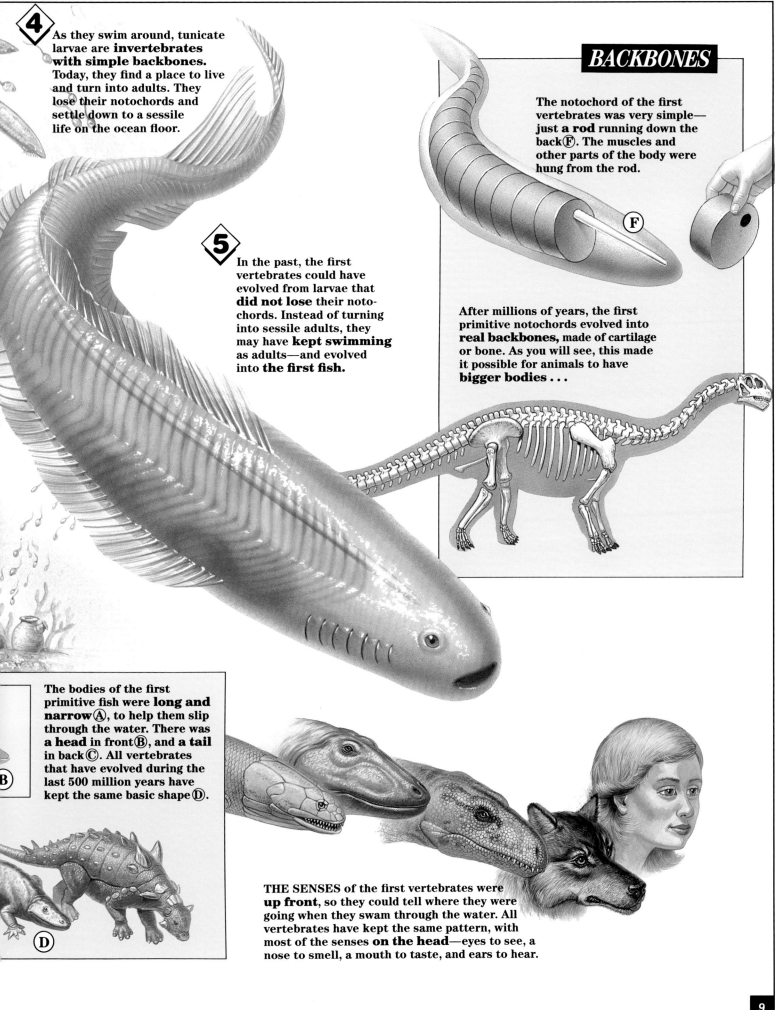

4 As they swim around, tunicate larvae are **invertebrates with simple backbones.** Today, they find a place to live and turn into adults. They lose their notochords and settle down to a sessile life on the ocean floor.

5 In the past, the first vertebrates could have evolved from larvae that **did not lose** their notochords. Instead of turning into sessile adults, they may have **kept swimming** as adults—and evolved into **the first fish.**

BACKBONES

The notochord of the first vertebrates was very simple— just **a rod** running down the back Ⓕ. The muscles and other parts of the body were hung from the rod.

After millions of years, the first primitive notochords evolved into **real backbones,** made of cartilage or bone. As you will see, this made it possible for animals to have **bigger bodies . . .**

The bodies of the first primitive fish were **long and narrow** Ⓐ, to help them slip through the water. There was **a head** in front Ⓑ, and **a tail** in back Ⓒ. All vertebrates that have evolved during the last 500 million years have kept the same basic shape Ⓓ.

THE SENSES of the first vertebrates were **up front,** so they could tell where they were going when they swam through the water. All vertebrates have kept the same pattern, with most of the senses **on the head**—eyes to see, a nose to smell, a mouth to taste, and ears to hear.

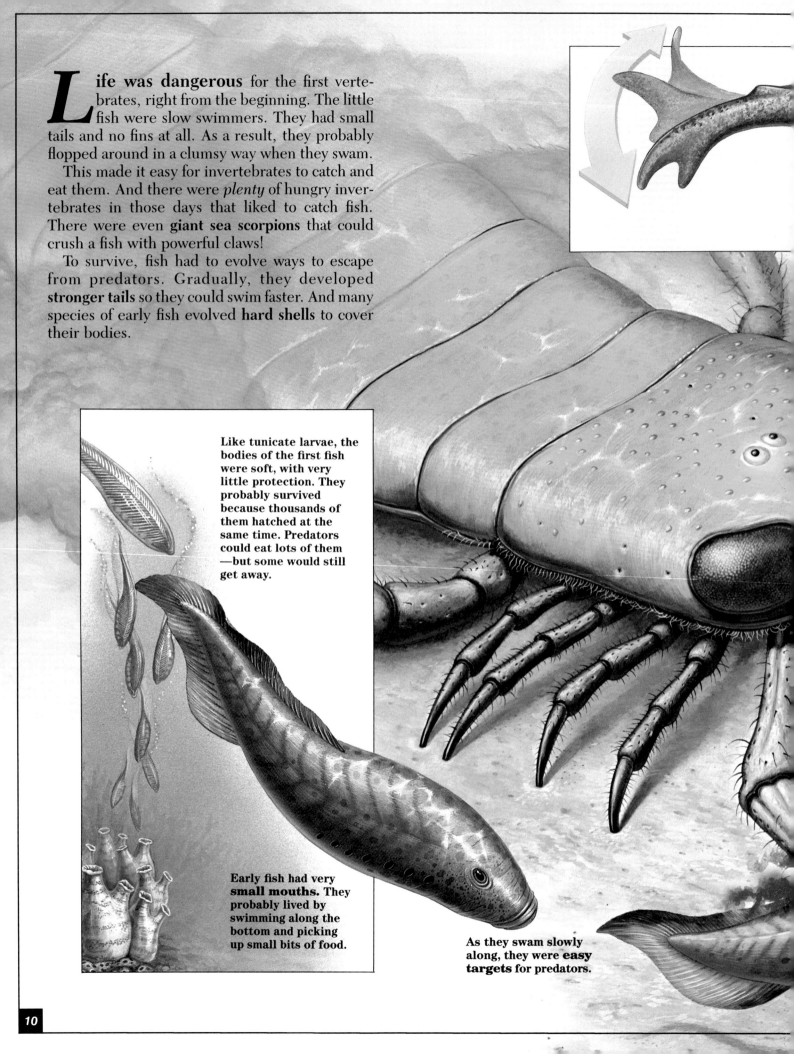

*L*ife was dangerous for the first verte-brates, right from the beginning. The little fish were slow swimmers. They had small tails and no fins at all. As a result, they probably flopped around in a clumsy way when they swam.

This made it easy for invertebrates to catch and eat them. And there were *plenty* of hungry inver-tebrates in those days that liked to catch fish. There were even **giant sea scorpions** that could crush a fish with powerful claws!

To survive, fish had to evolve ways to escape from predators. Gradually, they developed **stronger tails** so they could swim faster. And many species of early fish evolved **hard shells** to cover their bodies.

Like tunicate larvae, the bodies of the first fish were soft, with very little protection. They probably survived because thousands of them hatched at the same time. Predators could eat lots of them —but some would still get away.

Early fish had very **small mouths**. They probably lived by swimming along the bottom and picking up small bits of food.

As they swam slowly along, they were **easy targets** for predators.

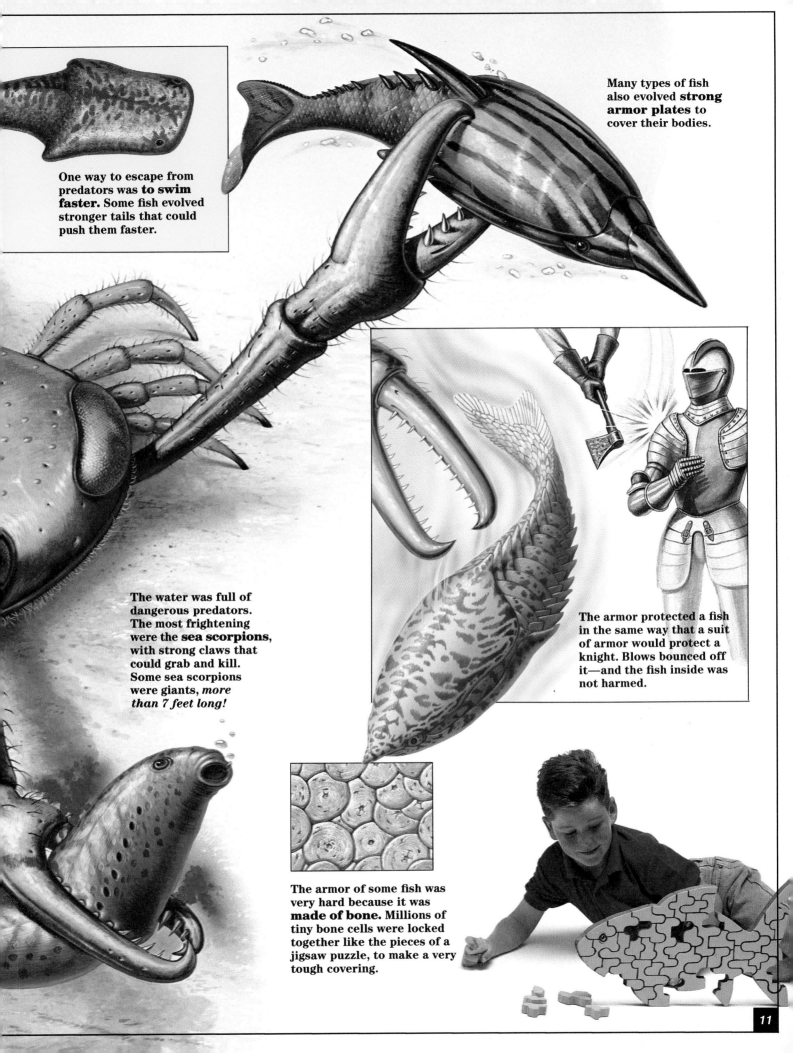

One way to escape from predators was **to swim faster.** Some fish evolved stronger tails that could push them faster.

Many types of fish also evolved **strong armor plates** to cover their bodies.

The water was full of dangerous predators. The most frightening were the **sea scorpions,** with strong claws that could grab and kill. Some sea scorpions were giants, *more than 7 feet long!*

The armor protected a fish in the same way that a suit of armor would protect a knight. Blows bounced off it—and the fish inside was not harmed.

The armor of some fish was very hard because it was **made of bone.** Millions of tiny bone cells were locked together like the pieces of a jigsaw puzzle, to make a very tough covering.

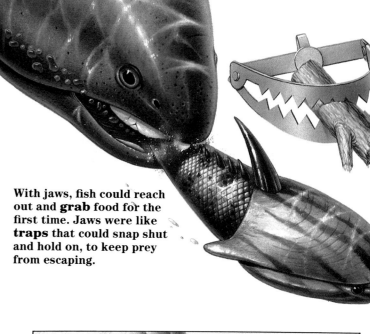

Getting more food was a very important problem for vertebrates, right from the start. As you know, the first fish were small. They had small and weak mouths without jaws. For this reason, they are called **jaw-less fishes.**

For millions of years, the bodies of jawless fishes **stayed small**—and this was probably because of their small mouths. They could not take in enough food to keep bigger bodies alive, so they couldn't evolve into larger fish.

This is why **fish "invented" jaws.** With jaws, they could grab and eat more food. and they could grow bigger. As you will see, some of them grew *very big indeed!*

With jaws, fish could reach out and **grab** food for the first time. Jaws were like **traps** that could snap shut and hold on, to keep prey from escaping.

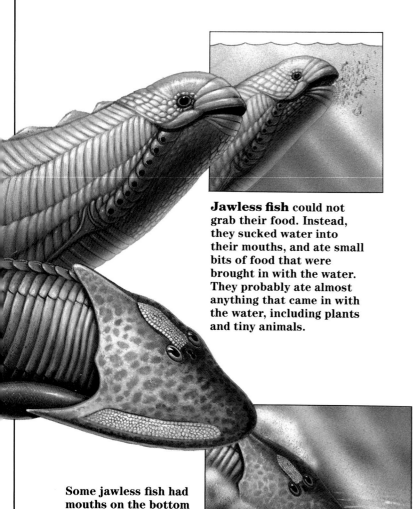

Jawless fish could not grab their food. Instead, they sucked water into their mouths, and ate small bits of food that were brought in with the water. They probably ate almost anything that came in with the water, including plants and tiny animals.

Some jawless fish had mouths on the bottom of their heads. They probably swam slowly along the bottom of the water, sucking up small pieces of food like **vacuum cleaners.**

Stronger jaws made it possible for fish to have **bigger mouths.** Some of these fish started chasing after **bigger food,** including other fish. In this way, some fish started to eat mostly meat. They became the first vertebrate **predators.**

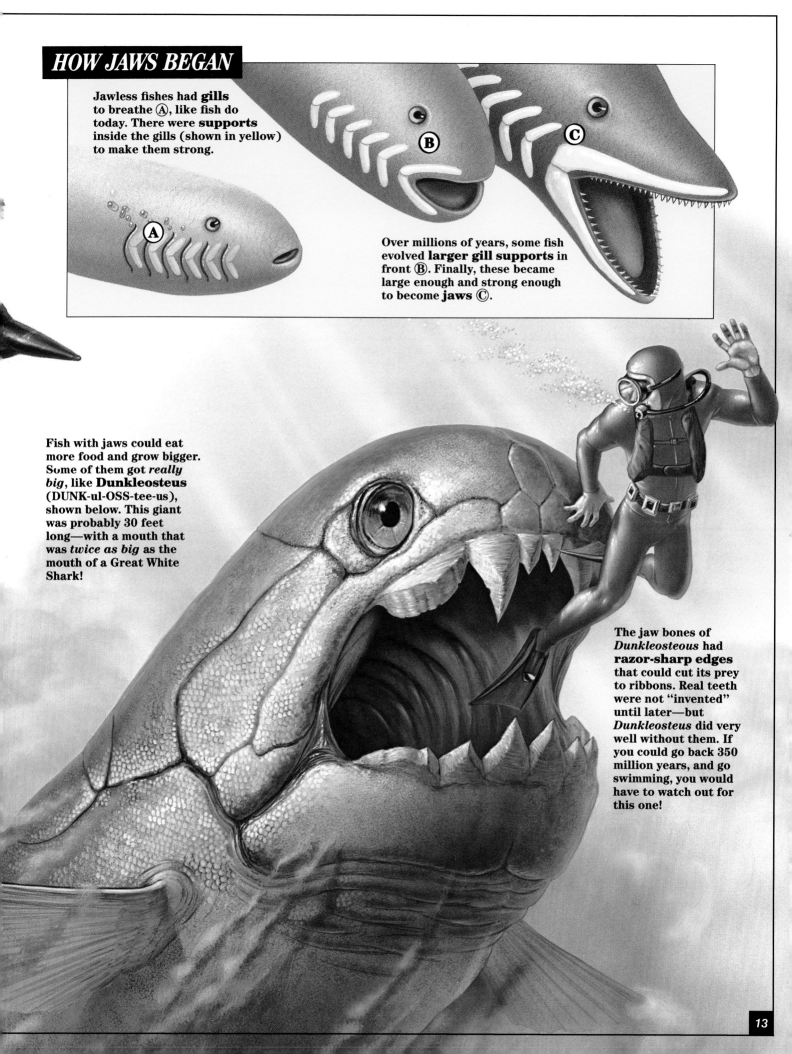

HOW JAWS BEGAN

Jawless fishes had **gills** to breathe Ⓐ, like fish do today. There were **supports** inside the gills (shown in yellow) to make them strong.

Over millions of years, some fish evolved **larger gill supports** in front Ⓑ. Finally, these became large enough and strong enough to become **jaws** Ⓒ.

Fish with jaws could eat more food and grow bigger. Some of them got *really big*, like **Dunkleosteus** (DUNK-ul-OSS-tee-us), shown below. This giant was probably 30 feet long—with a mouth that was *twice as big* as the mouth of a Great White Shark!

The jaw bones of *Dunkleosteous* had **razor-sharp edges** that could cut its prey to ribbons. Real teeth were not "invented" until later—but *Dunkleosteus* did very well without them. If you could go back 350 million years, and go swimming, you would have to watch out for this one!

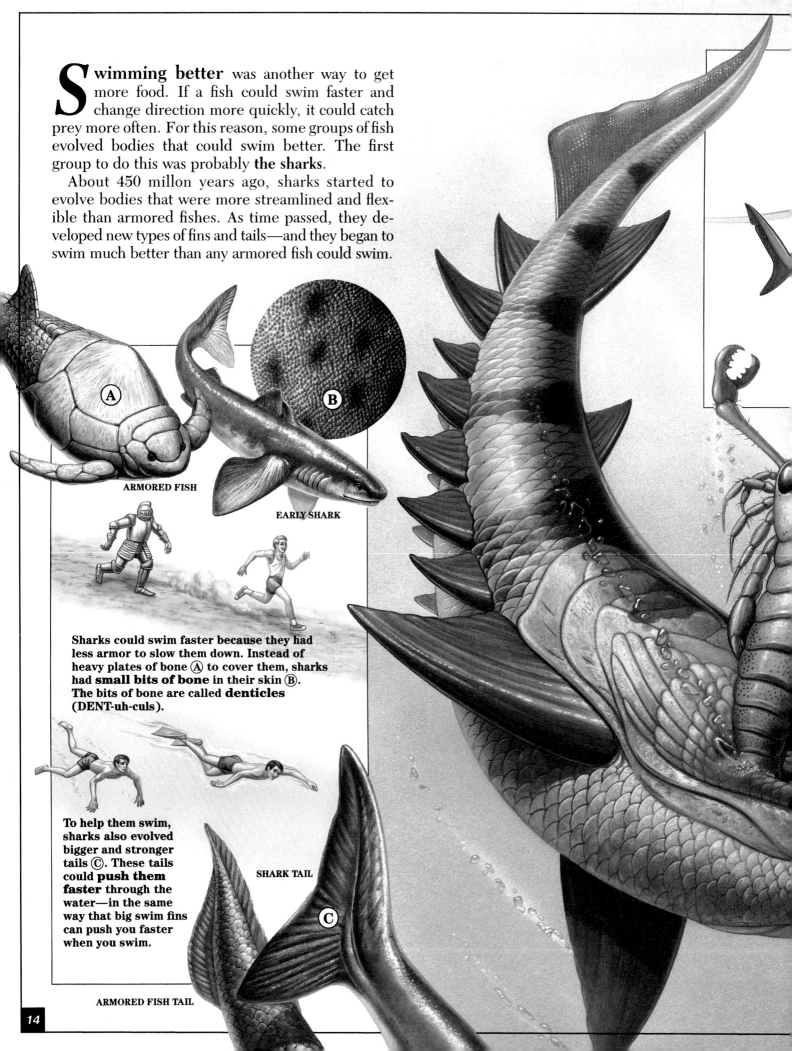

Swimming better was another way to get more food. If a fish could swim faster and change direction more quickly, it could catch prey more often. For this reason, some groups of fish evolved bodies that could swim better. The first group to do this was probably **the sharks**.

About 450 millon years ago, sharks started to evolve bodies that were more streamlined and flexible than armored fishes. As time passed, they developed new types of fins and tails—and they began to swim much better than any armored fish could swim.

ARMORED FISH

EARLY SHARK

Sharks could swim faster because they had less armor to slow them down. Instead of heavy plates of bone Ⓐ to cover them, sharks had **small bits of bone** in their skin Ⓑ. The bits of bone are called **denticles** (DENT-uh-culs).

To help them swim, sharks also evolved bigger and stronger tails Ⓒ. These tails could **push them faster** through the water—in the same way that big swim fins can push you faster when you swim.

SHARK TAIL

ARMORED FISH TAIL

FLYING IN THE WATER

The streamlined bodies of sharks made it possible for them to cut through the water much faster than armored fish. And sharks evolved **new types of fins** that could be used to change direction much faster.

2 For example, when the control surfaces on the wings of an airplane change position ⓓ, the airplane moves up or down.

1 The fins worked like the control surfaces on the wings and tails of airplanes. By **changing the position** of its fins, a shark could turn its body in many different directions.

3 In the same way, when the **pectoral** (PECK-tur-ul) **fins** of a shark ⓔ change position, the shark moves up or down.

Once a shark caught its prey, it could grab it with sharp teeth. Sharks were probably the first animals on earth to have **real teeth**.

REAL TEETH

Shark teeth probably evolved from **the denticles** in shark skin. As you can see, the denticles already look like small teeth ⓕ. In fact, the word denticle *means* "small tooth." The denticles along the edges of shark jaws ⓖ probably evolved into teeth over a long period of time—by simply getting bigger ⓗ and **BIGGER** ⓘ.

After millions of years, some sharks had teeth that were **really BIG**. One type of shark had teeth that were more than *6 inches long!*

GREAT WHITE SHARK TOOTH

ANCIENT SHARK TOOTH

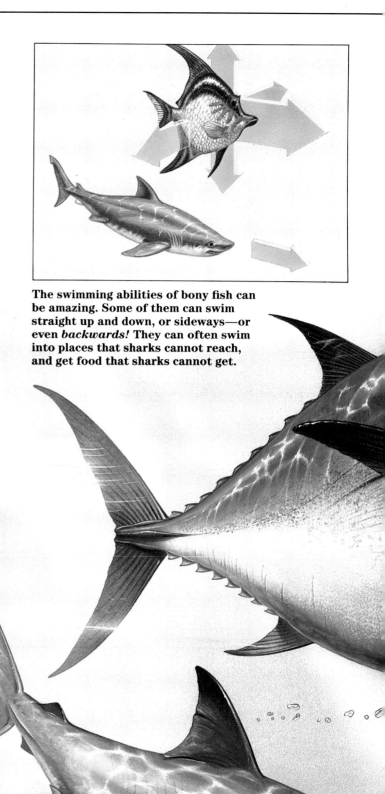

The best swimmers of all were another group of fish that started to evolve about the same time as sharks. This group is called **the bony fishes**—for the simple reason that they have more bone in their bodies than any other group of fish. The have **bony scales** on the outside of their bodies, and **bony skeletons** inside.

The ancestors of bony fishes lived in shallow ponds and streams about 450 million years ago. As time passed, many different kinds evolved. They spread out to find niches in all of the oceans, lakes, and streams of the world.

Today, they are the most successful vertebrate group on earth. More than *half of all vertebrate species* living on earth (including land animals) are bony fish. There are many more bony fish than there are people!

The swimming abilities of bony fish can be amazing. Some of them can swim straight up and down, or sideways—or even *backwards!* They can often swim into places that sharks cannot reach, and get food that sharks cannot get.

The scales on bony fish are really **a form of armor.** You remember that many early fish had large plates of heavy bony armor Ⓐ to protect them.

The first bony fishes still had thick armor Ⓑ. But the armor was broken up into **many small pieces.** These small armor plates were the first *fish scales*.

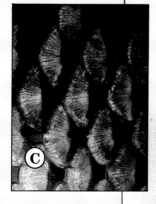

As time passed, new species with **thinner scales** evolved. Thinner scales weigh less and are more flexible—so the new fish were better swimmers. Today, most bony fish have very thin scales Ⓒ. But they are still **made of bone.**

THE FIRST LUNGS

1 Bony fish "invented" the first lungs Ⓓ. This probably happened because many of them lived **in shallow pools** of water Ⓔ. When the weather got hot, these pools would often start to **dry up** Ⓕ.

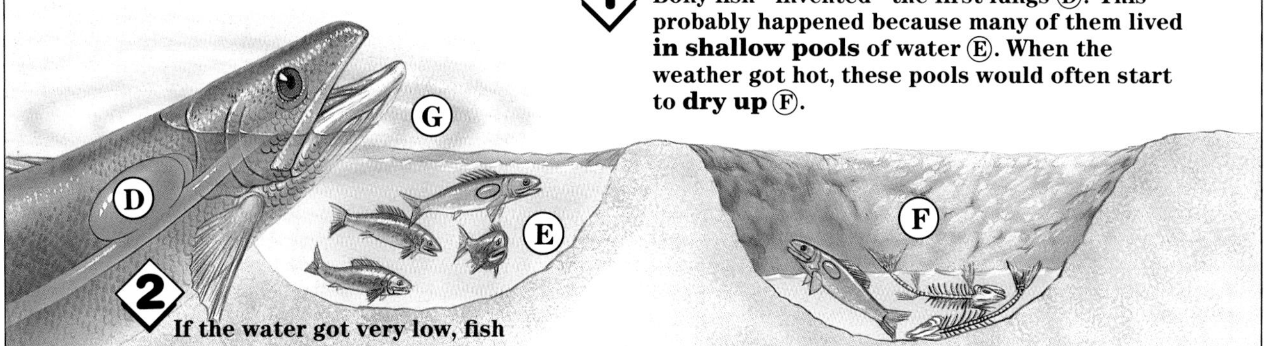

2 If the water got very low, fish that had to breathe through gills would die. But bony fish with gills *and* lungs could simply start breathing air directly Ⓖ, and **survive**.

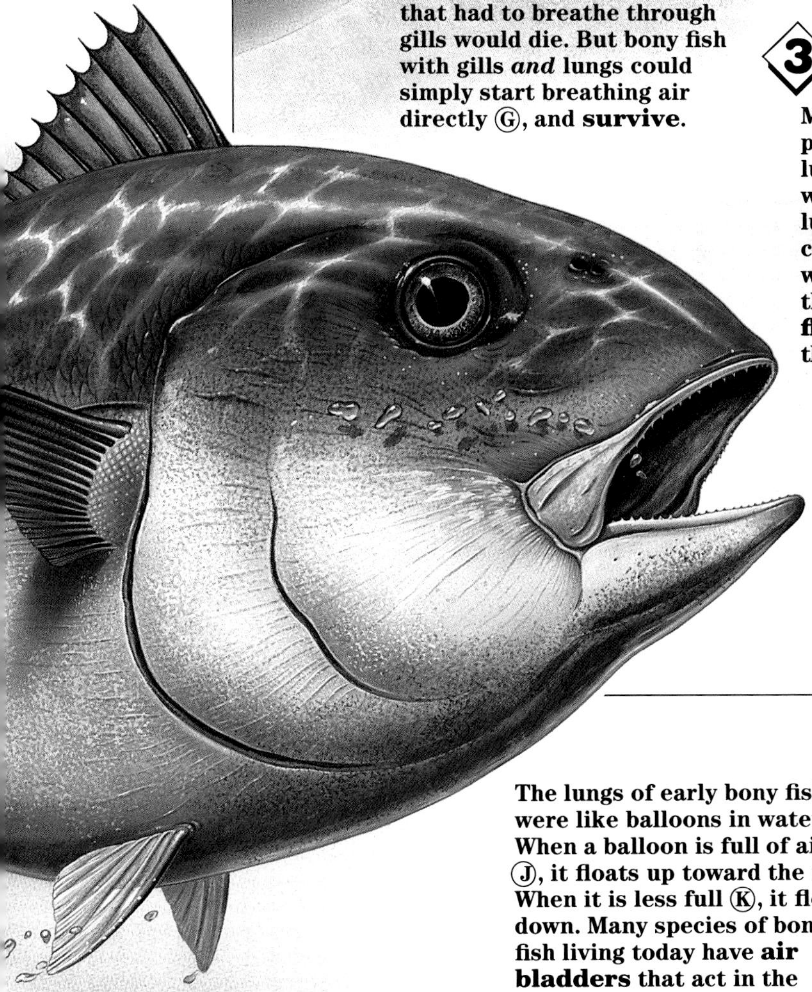

3 Many early bony fishes probably used their lungs in another way as well. By filling their lungs with air Ⓗ, they could **float up** in the water. And by emptying them Ⓘ, they could **float down**. The way this works is shown below.

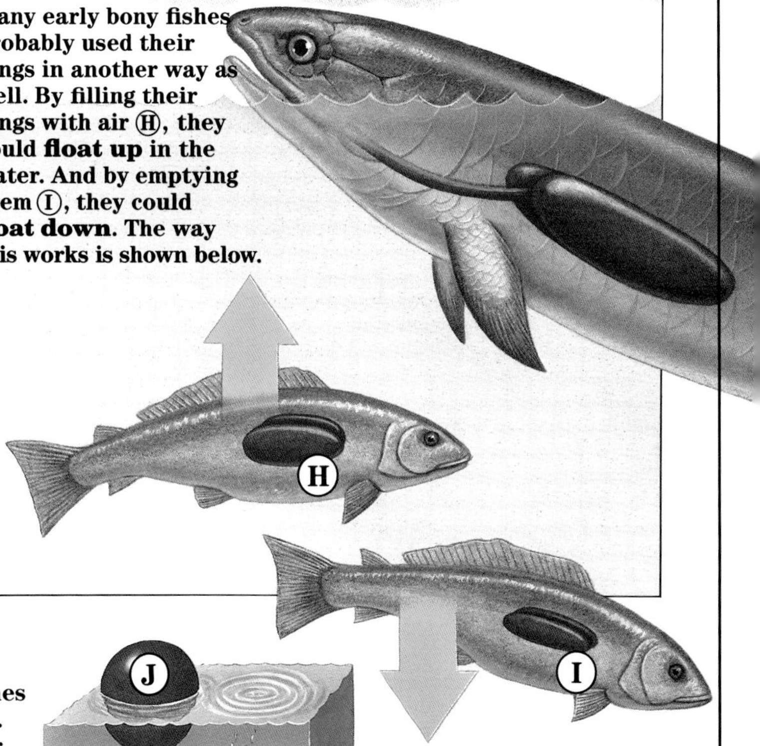

The lungs of early bony fishes were like balloons in water. When a balloon is full of air Ⓙ, it floats up toward the top. When it is less full Ⓚ, it floats down. Many species of bony fish living today have **air bladders** that act in the same way.

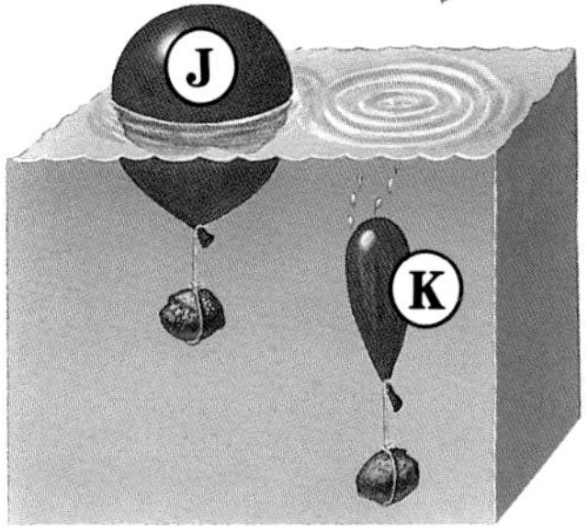

STRONG BONES

Bony fish were the first animals on earth to have skeletons made of **strong bone** Ⓛ. Armored fishes and sharks had skeletons made of a weaker material called **cartilage** Ⓜ.

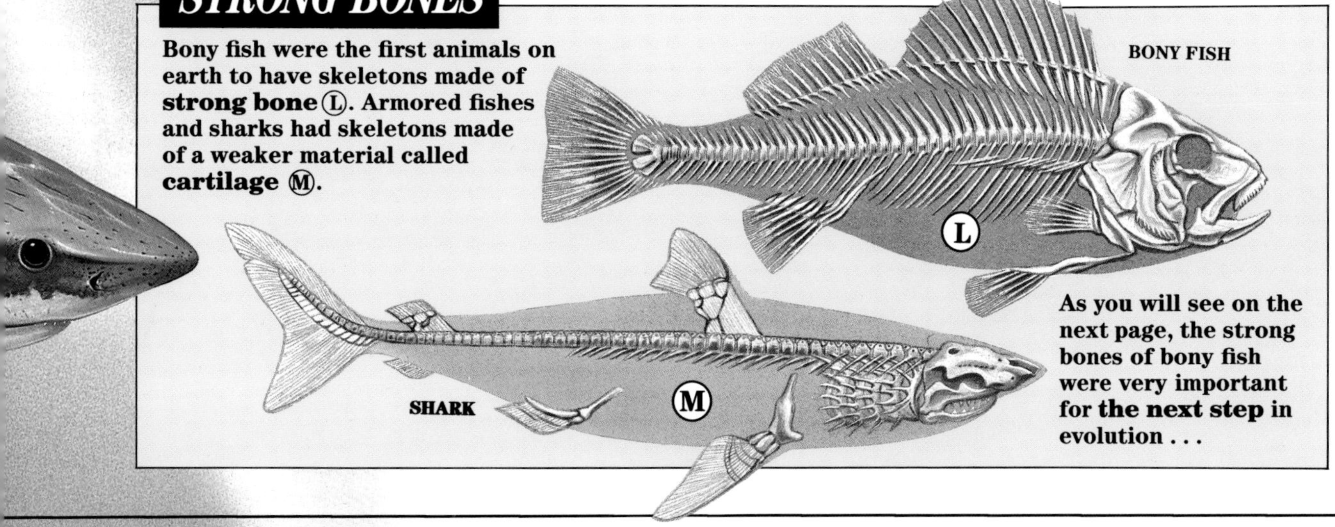

BONY FISH

As you will see on the next page, the strong bones of bony fish were very important for **the next step** in evolution . . .

SHARK

The strong bones and the lungs of some bony fish made it possible for something wonderful to happen. One group of bony fish called **lobe-finned fishes** developed very strong fins, with "fingers of bone" inside the fins to stiffen them. After a time, they were able to use their stronger fins **like legs**, to hold up their bodies. And then, they crawled out of the water and **up on the land**!

At first, they must have been clumsy out of the water. But they evolved stronger and stronger fins to move them around on land, and better lungs, too. After millions of years, they evolved into **amphibians**—the first vertebrates that could stay out of the water for long periods of time.

Why did the fish come out of the water? They were probably **looking for food**—like juicy insects. But maybe they were looking for *something else*, as you'll see below.

You may think that a fish could never use its fins to crawl out of the water. But there is a little fish living today that does it all the time. The fish is called a **mudskipper**.

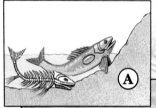

Some scientists say that the first fish that came out of the water were probably looking for more water. **(A)**

You remember that fish with lungs could survive in shallow pools that started to dry up **(A)**. If the pools dried up completely, the fish needed to find water **somewhere else**.

They may have discovered that they could use their fins on land to help them crawl to new pools of water **(B)**.

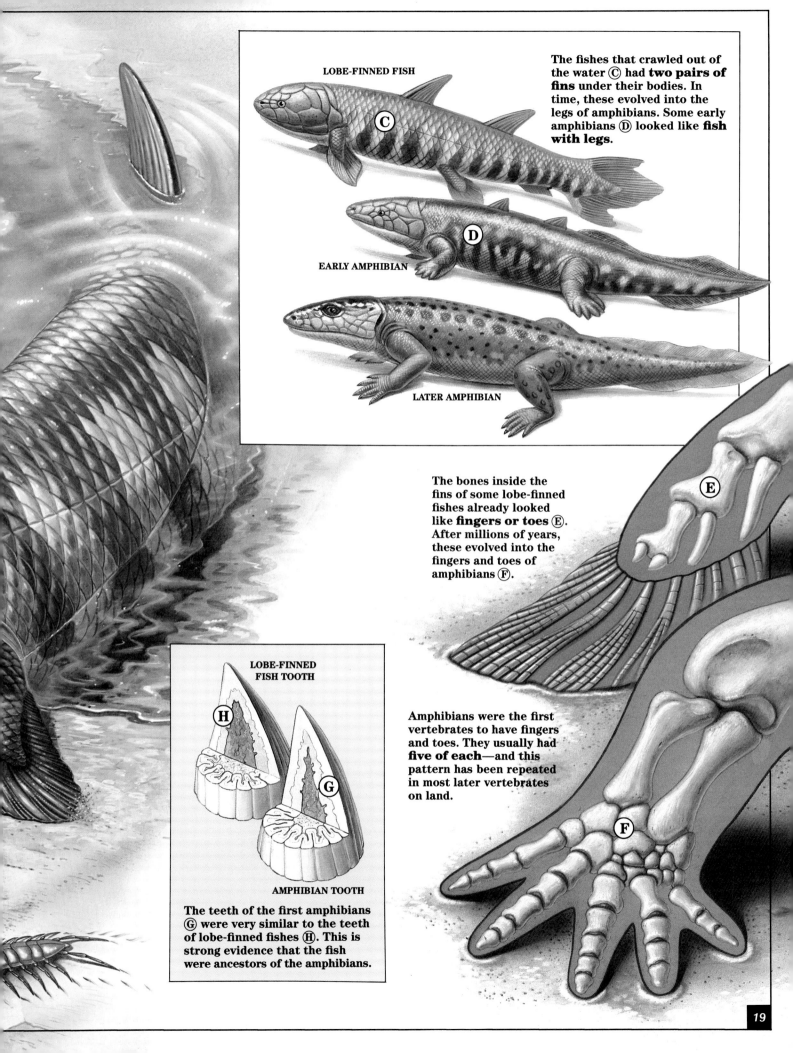

LOBE-FINNED FISH

C

The fishes that crawled out of the water C had **two pairs of fins** under their bodies. In time, these evolved into the legs of amphibians. Some early amphibians D looked like **fish with legs**.

D

EARLY AMPHIBIAN

LATER AMPHIBIAN

The bones inside the fins of some lobe-finned fishes already looked like **fingers or toes** E. After millions of years, these evolved into the fingers and toes of amphibians F.

E

Amphibians were the first vertebrates to have fingers and toes. They usually had **five of each**—and this pattern has been repeated in most later vertebrates on land.

F

LOBE-FINNED FISH TOOTH

H

G

AMPHIBIAN TOOTH

The teeth of the first amphibians G were very similar to the teeth of lobe-finned fishes H. This is strong evidence that the fish were ancestors of the amphibians.

A pattern for the bodies of all land vertebrates was set by the first fishes that crawled out of the water, millions of years ago. Ever since that time, all land vertebrates have been built on **the same general plan**.

Like the lobe-finned fishes, all land vertebrates have had strong **backbones**. And since the fishes crawled out on **four fins**, all land vertebrates have had **four limbs**—either four legs, or two arms and two legs.

Look around you at the land vertebrates that live in our world today. Whether you look at dogs, cats, birds, horses, or elephants—you will see the pattern repeated again and again.

As animals evolved, parts of the body often changed their functions. For example, the tails of fish are used to **push them through the water**. But the tails of reptiles and mammals helped them to **balance the weight** of their bodies.

CHANGING PARTS

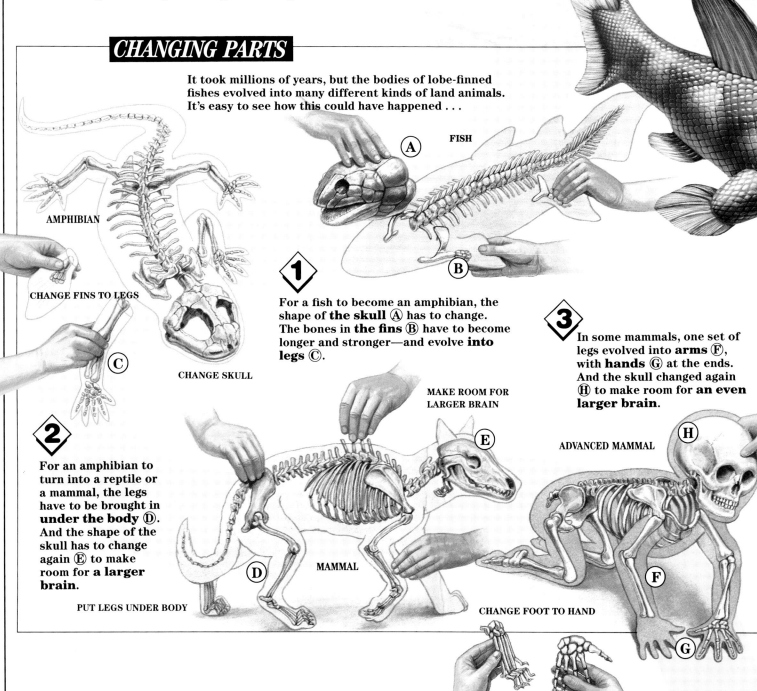

It took millions of years, but the bodies of lobe-finned fishes evolved into many different kinds of land animals. It's easy to see how this could have happened . . .

Ⓐ   **FISH**

AMPHIBIAN

CHANGE FINS TO LEGS

Ⓒ

CHANGE SKULL

Ⓑ

1

For a fish to become an amphibian, the shape of **the skull Ⓐ** has to change. The bones in **the fins Ⓑ** have to become longer and stronger—and evolve **into legs Ⓒ**.

3

In some mammals, one set of legs evolved into **arms Ⓕ**, with **hands Ⓖ** at the ends. And the skull changed again Ⓗ to make room for **an even larger brain**.

MAKE ROOM FOR LARGER BRAIN

Ⓔ

ADVANCED MAMMAL

Ⓗ

2

For an amphibian to turn into a reptile or a mammal, the legs have to be brought in **under the body Ⓓ**. And the shape of the skull has to change again Ⓔ to make room for **a larger brain**.

PUT LEGS UNDER BODY

Ⓓ   **MAMMAL**

CHANGE FOOT TO HAND

Ⓕ

Ⓖ

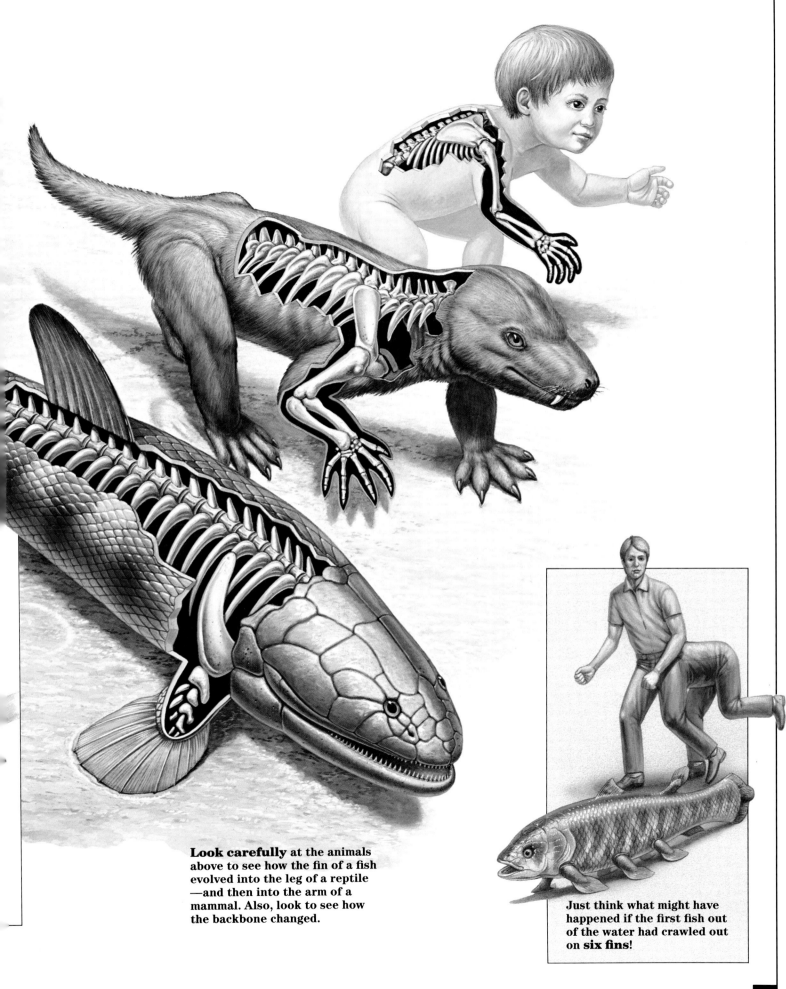

Look carefully at the animals above to see how the fin of a fish evolved into the leg of a reptile —and then into the arm of a mammal. Also, look to see how the backbone changed.

Just think what might have happened if the first fish out of the water had crawled out on **six fins**!

REMEMBER:

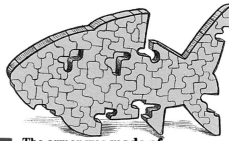

1 The first vertebrates evolved from **invertebrates**. This may have happened when **tunicate larvae** hatched from their eggs.

2 The larvae have **notochords**. Today, they swim around for a while, and then lose the notochords.

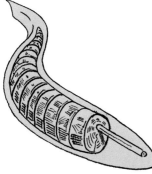

3 In the past, some larvae might have **kept their notochords**—and evolved into primitive fish.

4 After a long time, the notochords probably evolved into a real backbone—inside **the first real fish**.

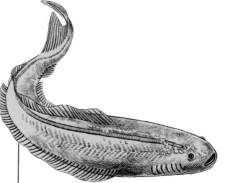

5 **Life was dangerous** for the first fish. There were many hungry invertebrates that wanted to eat them.

6 For this reason, many fish developed **hard armor** for protection.

7 The armor was **made of bone**. To make it strong, millions of bone cells were **locked together**—like the pieces of a jigsaw puzzle.

8 Early fishes had small mouths and **no jaws**. So they could only eat small bits of food.

9 The gill supports of some fish evolved into **jaws**—so they could catch **bigger food**.

10 With better jaws to catch more food, some armored fish became very BIG. **Dunkleosteus** was a giant over 30 feet long!

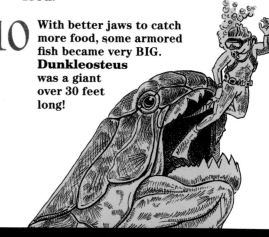

NEW WORDS:

Invertebrate
(IN-vert-uh-brayt)
Animal without a backbone.

Vertebrate
(VERT-uh-brayt)
Animal with a backbone.

Notochord
(NO-tow-cord)
Stiff rod that is a primitive backbone.

Larvae
(LAR-vee)
Baby animals that have a different shape than adults of the same species.

Tunicate
(TON-uh-kate)
Invertebrate animal with larvae that have notochords.

22

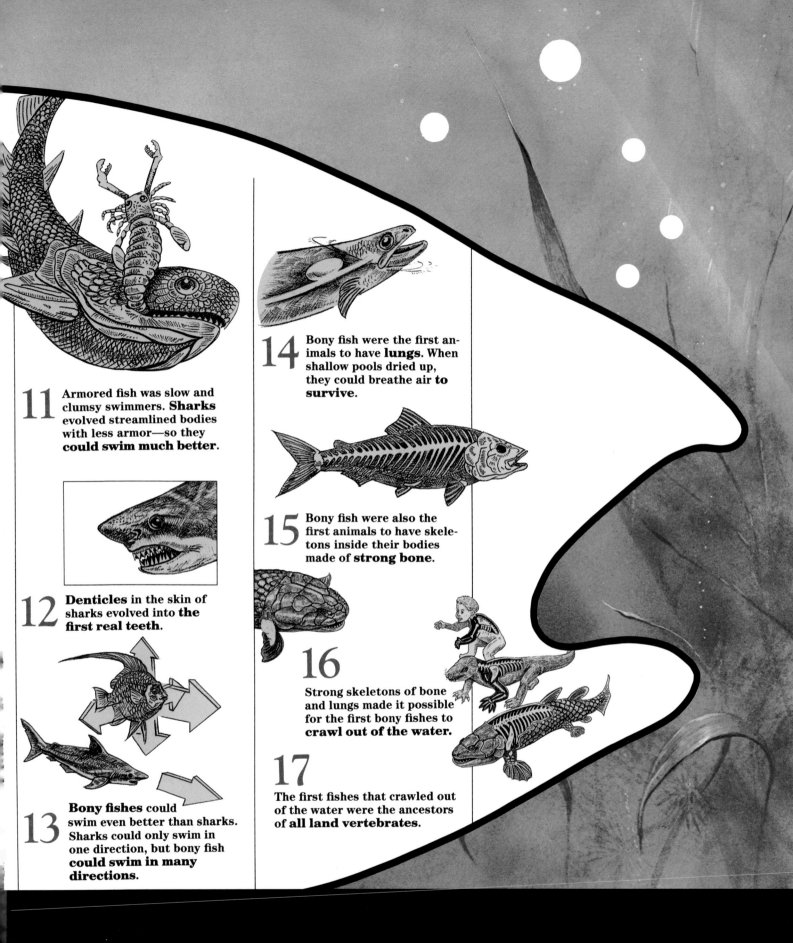

11 Armored fish was slow and clumsy swimmers. **Sharks** evolved streamlined bodies with less armor—so they **could swim much better.**

12 **Denticles** in the skin of sharks evolved into **the first real teeth.**

13 **Bony fishes** could swim even better than sharks. Sharks could only swim in one direction, but bony fish **could swim in many directions.**

14 Bony fish were the first animals to have **lungs.** When shallow pools dried up, they could breathe air **to survive.**

15 Bony fish were also the first animals to have skeletons inside their bodies made of **strong bone.**

16 Strong skeletons of bone and lungs made it possible for the first bony fishes to **crawl out of the water.**

17 The first fishes that crawled out of the water were the ancestors of **all land vertebrates.**

Dunkleosteus	**Denticle**	**Pectoral Fins**	**Cartilage**	**Lobe Fin**
(DUNK-ul-OSS-tee-us) Giant armored fish that lived 350 million years ago.	(DENT-uh-cul) Small piece of bone in the skin of a shark. A kind of armor.	(PECK-tur-ul) Fins on the bottom of a fish, toward the front of the body.	(CART-ul-lidj) What a shark's skeleton is made of. Not as hard as bone.	(LOWB fin) A kind of pectoral fin, with strong bones inside.

Index